POSTCARDS FROM ADULTHOOD

Postcards from Adulthood.

Take what is useful, leave the rest.

As a therapist, and person in process,
I often think about what messages could
be helpful to send to a younger version of
ourselves.

What if you could send a postcard from the
present, back to a painful point in the story?
Or to a place in yourself that still needs that
message today?

What resonates? What would you add? Use the
blank pages for your own words - the words
you needed to hear, or still need reminding
of — today.

One of the best parts of adulthood
is the chance to reexamine everything
we assumed and never questioned.
You get to choose now.

Monica

Your sensitivity is a gift not a liability.

Your complexity is a gift not a liability.

Don't edit yourself down to fit a box you were never meant to fit.

Allowing yourself to be misunderstood
may be one of the most important ways
you let yourself grow.

You are never the only one
who has experienced something.

You are therefore never alone.

Expectations placed on you
are not the same thing as what you want.

Take the time to learn the difference.

Trusting your own voice takes practice.

And, it is always a good time to start
practicing.

Understanding what was not your fault,
and what is not yours to carry,
is an essential part
of understanding your story.

And,
an essential part of healing.

The world doesn't need
one more version of the same thing.

Don't limit yourself to being
a version of anyone or anything.

The very things you were embarrassed about
may be what someone else needs to hear.

They will catch up to who you are becoming,
and if they don't,
that is also okay.

When we feel badly about ourselves,
we often shrink.
When we feel the truth of our loveliness,
we often expand.

I hope you believe the truth and expand.

What you are building may be
Imperceptible to other people.

That doesn't make it any less significant.

Keep building.

Good soil produces good growth.

Don't worry
if you are not growing
in a way others see yet.

So much of growth is
in preparing the soil.

Nurturing your growth
is often not loud.

Nurturing your growth,
is more often quiet.

It is making space for you to become.

The more permission we give ourselves
to be human,
to be human,
the less shame we feel.

One of the best parts of adulthood
is the chance to reexamine everything
we assumed and never questioned.

You get to choose now.

You were created for a purpose,
and no one else was consulted.

There wasn't a vote in a boardroom
about who you were allowed to be,
or who you should be.

Who you are,
and who you are becoming,
does not have to align with
someone else's expectations for you.

Healing requires exiting
the unhealthy relationship first.

Then the healing can begin.

Let's begin.

Under the tightrope of pleasing others
is the wide, flat ground of self acceptance.

It feels like a long fall,
but it's actually more like
a step down to sure and stable ground.

Expand as large as you can
when listening to the experiences of others.

Freehanded empathy.
Bountiful empathy.
Generous empathy.
Unsparing empathy.

For others.
For yourself.

Your capacity for thought,
creating,
relationships,
work,
hope
will vary.

This is normal.

Get curious instead of critical.

Words like "neighbor" get thrown around a lot.

But who is your neighbor?

Your neighbor is not identical to you.

You don't have to know someone well
to deeply grieve what they grieve.
You don't have to know someone well
to fight to protect them.
You don't have to be the same as someone
to listen to their experience.
You don't have to be the same as someone
to believe their experience.

This is called being a neighbor.

Be a neighbor.

You're upset because it's upsetting.
You're exhausted because it's exhausting.
You're worried because it's worrisome.
You're infuriated because it's infuriating.

Take a moment to validate your experience.

Just because someone in your life keeps
creating the same dramatic rollercoaster,
does not mean you have to get on.

Stand back,
get out of line,
don't get on the ride.

If "getting it right"
with an emotionally unpredictable person
was necessary in your upbringing,
the fear of "getting it wrong"
may be hard to shake.

Faith can look like...

Whispering "help" alone in the shower, when no one else can seem to help you.

Taking time to call your neighbor who talks a lot but is very lonely.

Saying no, because you are finally believing the truth of your belovedness—which means you don't have to over-give.

Trying again.

Listening.

Settling into the freedom of not being the expert on anything.

Waiting until you know which way to go, believing you will know.

Placing your worth only in being loved by God right now, and seeing each person with that same lens.

God is not impressed by my performance,
or worried by my doubt.

On Empathy:

You do not, nor do I,
have the right to tell someone
everything will be ok, or not to worry,
when you have never shared their lived
experience,
or face what they face.
If you don't have to worry because of your
privilege,
that has nothing to do with
someone else's reality.
Let's stop telling people how to feel,
and start holding space.

Sometimes the bravest thing
you can be with yourself,
is gentle.

When it comes to believing your worth in relationships,
replace question marks with periods.
You are not asking.
This is not a debate.

Some people will create a narrative for you
that has nothing to do with who you are,
but everything to do with their own
projections, defenses, and issues.
That is their story.
Not yours.

If your shoulders are tired...

Take a moment to validate everything that's on
your shoulders –
individually, collectively, from the past, and
for the future.

Your shoulders may be carrying loads they
didn't prepare for.

Shoulders that are tired don't need a
comparison to the load
of other shoulders.

Shoulders that are tired don't need a lecture
about how they shouldn't be tired.

Shoulders that are tired might need help
carrying the load.
Shoulders that are tired might need a shoulder
rub.
Shoulders that are tied probably need to rest.

And shoulders that are tired might need to
rest on someone else's for awhile.

If your heart is breaking,
if you are angry,
this means you are paying attention.

You are a home.

Consider with great care
who gets to inhabit that space.

Listening is not the same thing as relating.

In fact, trying to relate can keep us from
hearing one another.

You are never the expert on someone else's
experience.

And they are never the expert on yours.

Being in process is not a sign of failure,
it is a sign of life.

What are you carrying today?
It demands room,
and your attention.

It can feel so overwhelming to hold your
breath.
Sometimes you may not even realize you are
holding it.

But once you do,
it can feel like trying to hold the ocean back.
Futile.
And too hard to do.

You have to let it all move through you
and out.

The growth happening in you, and through
you, is often the most important part of the
"thing" you are doing...

You declare your worthiness,
when setting a new boundary.

You refuse to wast your brilliance and energy
on
making others comfortable,
when you use your voice.

You stop editing yourself down,
when you share your craft.

You experience your lovability,
when you let your guard down with a safe
person.

You experience yourself as who you are,
(and aren't you incredible),
when you stop trying to fit a box.

This is also a boundary:

Recognizing someone is not capable of
emotional safety,
and making decisions accordingly.

Don't argue with someone else's experience.

Don't argue with your own experience.

Curiosity without an agenda
feels a lot more like love.

Exhale thoughts for grownups...

You're not the only one feeling this way today.

The boundary you are setting is still valid,
whether they agree with you or not.

Not all delay is procrastination,
you may not have the energy today.
and that is ok.

Their misunderstanding of you
has nothing to do with who you actually are.

You were ok before they
judged or criticized you.
And you're still ok now.

A kindness given is no
guarantee of a kindness received.

But you can still be proud
of how you chose to be.

The combination of unrealistic expectations,
and not enough time of energy,
can falsely leave you feeling like a failure.
You're not a failure,
you might just need to adjust your
expectations.

It's ok to change your mind,
or not to know,
or not to know yet.

You don't have to play both roles in a
relationship.
Do your part, then rest.
This is also a boundary.

If your heart is feeling tender, remember:
Indifference is not strength.

Dear Monday Self,

Today is a reminder of what has not changed.

It is a reminder of what you're worried about,
sad about, or missing.

It's a reminder of what you wish was different.

The beginning of the week may not feel like a
fresh start,
but instead like a hard reminder.

I will be kind and slow with you Monday Self,
and with others in their Monday states.

Feeling is an unfolding.

Exhaling is an unfolding.

Unfold and take up space.

For all the things you didn't get to,
and were supposed to get to today.

For all the parts of you than dread, more than
celebrate, a new week.

Today was just another day that you matter,
in spite of what you didn't do.

If your day was heavy, let it be over.

If your heart is heavy, hold it or share it.

If your mind is heavy, rest it now.

Your worth,
your belovedness,
deserve investigation, celebration,
confirmation, and honoring.

This is your sacred work.
To agree with love.

Everything good in life requires some measure of vulnerability.

Everything good in my life has required vulnerability of me.

Honoring the parts of yourself that are
overwhelmed, worn out,
and have nothing left to give
is also love.

Taking the time
to listen to how you feel
is part of knowing yourself.

There is no reward for rushing.

Make space for not knowing.

Not knowing how you feel about something
is part of knowing yourself.

Sometimes change doesn't look like something
new.

Sometimes change is returning to what you
have forgotten.

Change is often a quiet whisper
of what you forgot,
and are so relieved to remember.

Sometimes change looks like returning.

If you've gotten lost,
return to the last place you know.

Finding peace is often messy.

Finding peace often includes disruption.

If you are working to find peace,
and you're in the middle of the disruptive part,
keep going.

It is not a sign you are on the wrong path.
Peace often includes disruption.

Exhaustion is cumulative.

You may feel different today
than you did at the beginning of this.

Allow your identity to be as complex as it
needs to be,
in order to be the truth.

Name what you did today, honor it.

Even if no one else celebrated it.

The size of the response
does not determine
the faithfulness of your action.

What someone thinks of you
doesn't actually determine anything about
you.

This is a boundary.

Whatever heavy thing you'r carrying tonight.
and however you had to bend in order to
shoulder it...

May you love,
not judge yourself,
for the ways you had to bend
to make it through this day.

What I would tell my younger self:

Disappointing people
may be one of the most important things
you allow yourself to do.

You may have
folded in on yourself
in order to please others,
creasing and hiding away corners of your
story.

Becoming yourself involves
unfolding all the parts you hid away.

Thoughts on boundaries:

You can't possibly meet all of their needs, and
your own.

You're ok even if they're not ok with you.

Your heart is worth more.
You don't have to do this anymore.

You are not obligated to maintain
an unhealthy bond.

You don't have to make this work.

You can be ok and disappoint them.

What else might you do with all that energy
focused on pleasing others?

Children become who we tell them they are.

And so do we.

Thoughts for those of us that are sensitive, or highly sensitive, during hard times:

In addition to your own worries, stress, and pain... You feel what others feel. You've never been accused of being stoic. You weren't wired with an ability to shut it all out.

And when so many in the world are hurting, well it is a lot.

And you feel it.

You feel the weight of the invisible stress. It isn't really invisible to you.

You wear it.

You might feel more anxious than usual, weighted down, distracted, irritable, or even depressed.

And there is so much noise. Metaphorically, and maybe literally in your home too. And all of that can overwhelm you.

It is ok to unplug for a moment.

And maybe a better way of putting it is, it is necessary for you to unplug. You must shut the system down for a bit here and there and let all of your really powerful feelers rest.

Let them rest. Because you are grieving with the grieving, hurting with the hurting, angry with the injustice, anxious with the fearful, stressed with the worried.

When you are sensitive, you are "with" others so much, whether you know them or not. And when it feels like the whole world is hurting or worried, you can become overwhelmed.

Just like any superpower, your ability to feel what others feel needs to be understood and protected. You can't give what you don't have.

Don't edit yourself
out of your voice.

Everyone has something to say.

It doesn't have to be the newest,
or greatest,
to need to be said.

What if those words you really needed
were never spoken or written.

When it gets really noisy outside,
it can get really noisy inside.

If you're having trouble focusing,
difficulty feeling motivated,
if you're exhausted,
tired,
tender.

You're just awake.

Don't forget the context of what you're living
through.

We often turn on,
and blame ourselves,
when we underestimate of forget context.

Layer on an extra layer of
grace and self-kindness
for each thing that feels hard today.

It's often a series of compromises,
none bigger than the last,
that disconnects you from yourself.

And the good news is –
it's often a series of small decisions,
none bigger than the last,
that leads you back home to yourself.

Humanity wins when we stop
making our own experience the lens
through which we interpret the world.

Expand as large as you can
when listening to the experiences of others.

Sometimes we confuse out exhaustion
with not being good enough.

May we untangle the two,
and let ourselves rest.

What I would tell my younger self:

They don't necessarily know better than you,
they're just louder.

Change is not a tidy business.

We're never surprised at the mess
of renovating a house.

Why would renovating ourselves
be any less complicated?

May what I did today be enough.

In hopes of serving my tomorrow,
may I accept my limitations and rest.

Insight is often quiet, not loud.

Change is a practice, not a decision.

When you feel anxious you're falling behind,
clarify who it is you're trying to keep up with.

Because you can't fall behind
on your own road.

When you are performing,
you may also be quietly agreeing
that you're not good enough as you are.

Kindness is not passive.

Kindness refuses to bend
to hatred, jealousy, disconnection,
comparison, apathy, and ruthless hustle.

It is more important to be kind
than to be great.

I rest when I stop trying to be anything other
than who I am,
because it is good enough.

I rest when I remember I am loved.

And in that rest I silently agree,
these are the truths that anchor me,
and everything else can wait.

What I would tell my younger self:

You weren't created to please them.
You weren't created to over-accommodate.
You weren't created to edit yourself down.
You weren't created to be small so they're
comfortable.
You weren't created to filter *yourself* through
their lens.

You were created for a purpose,
and they weren't consulted.

You have permission
to leave the room.

Kindly exit the conversations,
internally and externally,
that are hurting you.

Feeling more than one thing at a time isn't
confusion,
it is normal.

The thing is, that we rarely, if ever,
feel only one thing at a time about
a day, a situation, a role, or a relationship.

Your Inner Committee,
the one you run decisions by in your mind,
didn't get there by accident.

If the voices aren't kind,
it is time for a re-election.

Admirable people are often not famous.

They are quietly consistent.

They do hard,
non-glamorous things over and over.

They rarely get the praise other people get
for less meaningful work.

Becoming involves unbecoming.
laying down all the names
that were assigned to you
that don't fit anymore,
or maybe never did.

Leaving your hands free
to pick up what is true.

Listening includes recognizing:

You are never the expert
on someone else's experience.

We learn to recognize a voice
by listening to it.

Including your own.

Make your internal world so lovely
that it is a warm place for you to return to,
and a loving place to invite others into.

We don't just grow up.

We grow wider, deeper, surer, stronger.

Letting go of:

Trying to shape my experience
to match your story about it.

One size fits
no one
nothing
ever.

Breaking new grounding your own life is
loving and sacred work.

It is not overnight work.

Take your time, rest,
and keep going.

Loving reminder:

All the most important things
you've done in your life,
you weren't sure how to do right at first.

But you showed up anyway.

Allowing yourself the space
to sit with painful feelings
also allows the space
for grace to show up.

A plant doesn't grow because it
concentrates really hard,
or beats itself up.

A plant grows with
the right conditions,
and so do we.

Who is narrating your story?

Is she kind?

What I would tell my younger self:

Just let it be.
Let it be that you're different than they
expected.
You can handle this discomfort.

Some of your biggest growth
may be quiet.

Silent footsteps
only you can see.

Breakthroughs
don't
announce themselves beforehand.

Keep going.

You don't need to have
something for everyone.

You are not a buffet.

*A letter to my anxious friend during tragic and
scary news:*

Pain isn't the same as fear.
But fear can be more familiar, so we stay
there.

We get scared. Everything is not ok.
And we hate it when people tell us it is, don't
we?

And everything doesn't happen for a reason.
What a hollow attempt to fix suffering. But
everything does happen.

And when heroes fall, or threats rage, we feel
our fragility. But it's always there. We often
numb ourselves to the constant tragedies
happening, and that many in the world are
much more vulnerable than us at all times.

The knock on the door with bad news for our
neighbor, near or far, breaks the illusion of
comfort. And breaks our heart if we are paying
attention.

And pay attention. Let it break your heart. The anxiety may be you trying to keep yourself from feeling that pain.

Numbing isn't the solution, it fools us into believing our door is locked, secure. There is no lock on the door between us and pain. And we all share the same door.

Tragedy reminds us the door is open after all, and to hold onto each other through the doorway of pain. Because we'll all pass through it.

It's all so fragile.
Hold onto each other.
Anchor in God.

The wind, cold and harsh, is the same air that is warm and soft, we have to feel it all to feel the good. We can't selectively numb. I hate wind, and given a choice would feel nothing. But then I'd miss everything. Feel the wind, weep with others, pray, help. We can move through anxiety as we feel and help.

Closing the door
on what is not for me
helps me define my space.

We confuse ease with confirmation,
and difficulty with doubt.

Easy doesn't mean it is right,
and hard doesn't mean it is wrong.

Most worthy tasks are going to cost us a lot.

Work is an expression of your gifts,
your commitment, your dreams,
your love, your needs.

Not your worth.

It is an expression,
not a definition.

About Monica DiCristina:
Monica DiCristina is a Licensed Professional Counselor with more than a decade of experience in individual and couples therapy. She walks with people as they process difficult experiences, helping to bring healing to their relationship with themselves and others. Through her podcast, writing, speaking, and counseling work, Monica carries out her heartfelt mission to guide and collaborate with others in their process of becoming who they were made to be.

Website: monicadicristina.com
Instagram: @monicadicristina
Podcast: Still Becoming
Kids Podcast: Still Becoming Kids

Made in the USA
Coppell, TX
09 September 2021

62079083R00069